Essential Question
How do animals help each other?

Penguins All Around

by Donna Loughran

Penguins live in groups.

Look at the penguins walk! Penguins waddle because they cannot fly.

penguins

wings

feet

Look at the penguins swim!
Two wings and webbed feet
help them swim.

Penguins are good swimmers.

The penguins <u>dive</u> into the blue sea. They look for food.

In Other Words jump into the water. En español: *tirarsen al agua.*

krill

sea

Penguins eat small fish or krill. Krill look like small shrimp.

5

seal

Seals eat penguins.

Penguins live in big groups. This helps them stay safe from danger.

White feathers help penguins hide in the snow. Black feathers help them hide in the sea.

Penguins are hard to see in the water.

(t) Ben Cranke/The Image Bank/Getty Images, (b) Kevin Schafer/Stone/Getty Images

Some penguins live in very cold places. They huddle together to stay warm.

Kim Westerkov/Photographer's Choice/Getty Images

Penguins stand close together.

nest

This penguin rests in a grass nest.

Penguins make nests with a partner. The nests are made of stones. Other nests are made of grass.

See the egg! When will it open? We will wait and see.

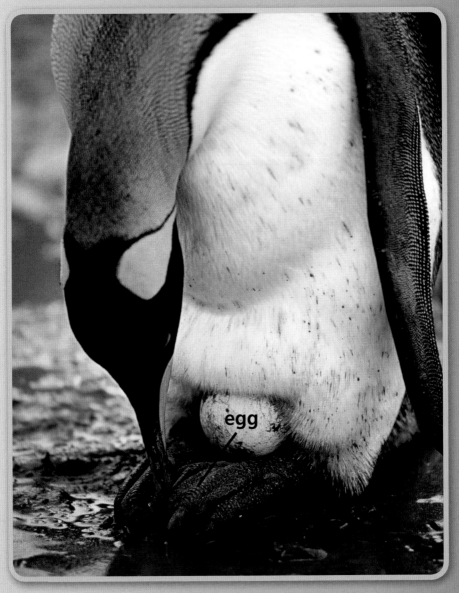

egg

This penguin is keeping its egg warm.

The baby chicks <u>hatched</u>!
Mom and Dad care for
the babies.

baby chick

These chicks have
fluffy gray feathers.

This penguin feeds
her chick.

<u>**In Other Words**</u> are born. En español: *nacieron.*

Now the baby penguins
are big! They can dive into
the sea. They will make
new nests.

Respond to Reading

Retell

Use the chart to help you retell *Penguins All Around.*

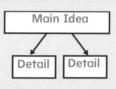

Text Evidence

1. Look at page 5. What do penguins eat? Main Idea and Key Details

2. Look at page 7. How do penguins stay warm? Main Idea and Key Details

3. Is *Penguins All Around* a real story? Why? Genre

Genre Nonfiction

Compare Texts
Read about how animals work together.

Animals Work Together!

elephants

Elephants live in groups. They work together.

Dolphins live in groups. They stay safe together.

dolphins

A group of dolphins is called a pod.

image100/PunchStock/Getty Images

14

A group of ants is called a colony.

Ants live in big groups, too! They build nests and look for food together.

Make Connections
Look at both stories. How are penguins like the other animals you read about? Text to Text

Focus on
Science

Purpose To compare two animals

What to Do

Step 1 ▶ Work with a partner. Draw a chart like this one.

Alike	Different
live in groups	only one can swim

Step 2 ▶ Pick two animals that you read about.

Step 3 ▶ Write one way the animals are alike. Write one way they are different.

Conclusion Tell a friend about your chart.

16